GAZA
HELD IN TIME

A Tapestry of Two Lives

Tareq AlSourani & Yara Nasser

Daraja Press

Published by
Daraja Press
https://darajapress.com
Wakefield, Quebec, Canada

Cover art: Shareef Sarhan

Shareef Sarhan is a Palestinian visual artist, photographer, and designer. He is a founder of Windows" Gaza Contemporary Art Group. He has published two books, *Gaza War* and *Gaza Lives*.

ISBN 9781998309955 (soft cover)
ISBN 9781998309962 (ePub)

Library and Archives Canada Cataloguing in Publication

Title: Gaza held in time : a tapestry of two lives / Tareq AlSourani & Yara Nasser.
Names: AlSourani, Tareq, author. | Nasser, Yara, author.
Identifiers: Canadiana (print) 20250243385 | Canadiana (ebook) 20250246392 |
    ISBN 9781998309955
(softcover) | ISBN 9781998309962 (EPUB)
Subjects: LCSH: AlSourani, Tareq. | LCSH: Nasser, Yara. | LCSH: Young adults—
    Gaza Strip—Gaza— Biography. | LCSH: Israel-Hamas War, 2023-—Biography. |
    LCSH: Gaza—Biography. | LCGFT: Autobiographies.
Classification: LCC DS119.771 .A47 2025 | DDC 956.94/3055092535—dc23

To the People of Gaza

Written by four hands, from inside and outside Gaza as if a rope also physically kept the two narrators tied together. There is no page that does not simultaneously strike the reader's reason and heart, both in the transmission of pain and injustice and in the memory of a beauty that those who have known Gaza can confirm, despite the siege and periodic Israeli attacks. No surrender to pity, rather a severe refusal of any compassion and hypocrisy that undermines the dignity of one's people.

If calling a work that exudes pain a jewel does not offend the authors, I allow myself to say that this little book is a true jewel.

– **Patrizia Cecconi**, author of *Vagando di erba in erba, racconto di una vacanza in Palestina*

Tareq AlSourani and Yara Nasser, both still teenagers, provide an extraordinary evocation of the endless fear, loss, humiliation and horror of life in Gaza over the last twenty months. Still in Gaza, Yara's poetry captures the numbness of those managing to survive, like "dead people walking." Crossing into Egypt, Tareq expresses the guilt and anguish of escape, while loved others remain.

In writing that is as profound as it is stunning, both teenagers write of the Gaza they loved, pre-invasion, desperately trying to hold on to a faint hope for the future, while knowing they must find a way of remembering, however painful, when memory is resistance. Their words should haunt us forever.

– **Lynne Segal**, writer, academic and activist, Birkbeck, University of London, UK

Devastating… these could be our children. A brave and necessary book.

– **Yahia Lababidi**, Palestinian poet and author of *Palestine Wail*

A greatly moving essay that expresses the belief that not only Palestinians can survive without surrendering and that buildings may fall, but voices do not.

– **Paul Aarts**, lecturer in international relations and Middle East politics at the University of Amsterdam

This book is a moving, intimate account of what it means to try and survive erasure. To remain true to self, to friendship, to love, in the face of unimaginable cruelty. It is by writing this tender, deeply human testimony that Tareq and Yara defy this crime of erasure committed against them, indict it even. A hugely courageous act.

– **Rinke Verkerk**, Dutch journalist and writer, *De Correspondent*

FOREWORD

Two young voices rise from the heart of devastation—Tareq AlSourani and Yara Nasser—two students who, by their own brave initiative, chose to write not just of war, but of memory, survival, and the fragmented light that still breaks through Gaza's darkest skies. Their words are not merely a chronicle of pain; they are a declaration of presence. In their courage and clarity, I see the promise of a generation that refuses erasure—a generation of brilliant Palestinian minds whose resilience, depth, and intellect are nothing short of extraordinary. I am humbled and proud to witness their ascent.

In times of great sorrow, the act of creation becomes sacred. To write, to compose, to shape grief into art, is not indulgence—it is medicine for the soul. Whether through literature, painting, music, or innovation, the act of expression allows the wounded spirit to breathe again. This book, with its tender rage and poetic truth, is a reminder that art is not only a tool of resistance but also a quiet act of self-salvation. In each page, we witness the human capacity to endure—and to transform suffering into something that speaks, heals, and dares to remain.

The world must listen—truly listen—to what Palestinian children and adolescents have endured. These are not abstract victims in distant reports; they are storytellers, thinkers, and dreamers who carry a burden too vast for their years. Their testimonies demand more than sympathy; they demand understanding. Through their words, the world is invited beyond headlines and into the living, breathing heart of tragedy—a tragedy that continues, unpaused, but one that must no longer be ignored.

Yet even here, among the ruins, the book leaves us not with despair, but with something more powerful: hope. Hope not as sentiment, but as architecture—as vision. In the quiet resilience of these young writers, a door opens toward what is possible. A future still stands—unwritten, unbroken—waiting to be shaped by hands that have known loss and still choose to build. Let this book be not only a record of sorrow, but a lantern toward what comes next.

Aref F. Husseini
Author

Aref Husseini is a distinguished novelist from Jerusalem. He is the author of an inspiring trilogy—*Sabbat Goy* (2012), *Relative Taboo* (2017), and *Half-Ashkenazi* (2024)—three novels that vividly illuminate the challenges and realities faced by Palestinians in Jerusalem. Through these works, Husseini offers a unique and insightful perspective on their lived experiences. In addition to his literary contributions, Aref Husseini is the founder and CEO of the Al Nayzak Foundation for Education and Scientific Innovation.

PREFACE

We are two young people from Gaza. Grew up under the same sky, walked the same streets, and heard the same sounds of birds and drones. But war changed our story paths.

One of us left Gaza, with agony, after experiencing multiple evacuations and the trauma of leaving home to nowhere, then heading to a forced diaspora.

One stayed behind, with all the challenges, miseries, famine, and extreme horror.

We never intended to write a book together. But when everything around us was falling apart, writing became the only way to hold onto what remained.

Our voices tell a story from different angles, trying to reflect, as much as possible, the feelings of the young people of Gaza. As we have faced different encounters, this book is written by two voices. We kept them separate on purpose—because war did not treat us the same, and Gaza has never been one story.

We wrote this so Gaza would not fade into headlines and statistics, so the lives lived and lost would not vanish silently. If our words shift in tone—sharper, softer, slower—let them. That shift is the truth. Let it shake you. Let it remind you that Gaza is not one story. It never was.

This book is not a political analysis or historical commentary. It is a conversation about survival, guilt, hope, and memory. It is about life as we lived it, lost it, and remember it. It is a pulse.

The war didn't ask if we were ready to write. It handed us rubble and silence—and told us to make sense of it.

Gaza is not gone. But parts of us are.

This is what remains.

Tareq's Account: In Gaza and Beyond

On the evening of October 7, 2023, I was looking forward to a family barbecue by the Gaza beach, enjoying the gentle late-autumn sunshine. Going to our wonderful beach always felt special, a moment of pure happiness for me. The beach was located near Deir Al-Balah, where the sand was soft and golden, and the waves danced quietly along the shore. It was not a beach with dunes or high cliffs, just a flat stretch of coast, simple but full of life. Families brought their own grills, children chased each other near the water, and the breeze always carried the scent of the sea mixed with roasted corn.

But the next morning, strange sounds woke us. The awful reality of renewed fighting was back. As I overheard my parents talking about cancelling our plans, I found myself just counting, trying to steady my breath, wondering, "When will it stop? Will we ever have a season of peace?"

This was the seventh war of my life. And somehow, it felt worse. It felt enormous. Gaza shook under intense fire, the sky screaming louder than ever before. It was deafening, like a thousand thunderstorms falling all at once. Like the end of the world had come, and we were living it minute by minute.

Soon, leaflets fell from the sky, ordering us to leave. Not just our house, but our whole life—our memories, our street, my room painted with dreams of becoming a computer expert. Leaving home that day felt like losing myself. Yet we left, again and again, southward, each move bringing more loss, more fear, more darkness.

I've cooked over open wood fires, carried water from the sea, crossed borders trembling, and lost people I loved deeply. My aunt and her children vanished under the rubble. My father remained trapped behind closed borders, helping others while we fled to Egypt. And still, every night I close my eyes, I'm there—back in Gaza, standing in the smoke and ruin.

Now I write from outside, from a place where safety feels strange, where peace carries a weight of guilt. I write because silence feels like betrayal. Because every day, I still hear Gaza calling, and I must answer.

This is my voice—one of survival through departure, memory, and the hope that somewhere in these pages, the home I left behind might live forever.

Yara's Account: A Prolonged Witness

When Tareq reached out again to continue our work on this book, then asked me to write an introduction that reflects my current experience since we are writing this apart.

I was sitting in the middle of a city under evacuation orders. The Israeli Occupation Forces had just demanded the displacement of thousands. I was in the middle, again.

Tareq told me to write with enthusiasm, as he always did. I set aside my physics problems and began to write down whatever was on my mind. Still confused, but I promise this: even if Tareq asked for a hundred pages, he would've received them easily.

Tareq left Gaza. I couldn't. That's what this book is: two versions of survival trying to meet on the same page.

I understand that we two offer two different writing styles. But that's the contrast. That's the point. I'm honored to introduce my contribution to this project, hoping it will help set the intellectual and moral tone for everything that follows.

We want to deliver a full picture of what it is like to live, think, and remember under siege.

Still, we are not describing or explaining Gaza. We are writing to remember it as it is, as we lived it, as we survived it, and as we continue to survive it.

The thing is, when you are born under siege, literature stops feeling metaphorical. It becomes a mirror. You write because you don't remember the first time you heard the drone. You only remember how normal it became.

And so here comes one of my many questions: How do you mourn something that still exists? How do you grieve a home that keeps being erased, not all at once, but piece by piece?

I distinctly remember the day I read *The Kite Runner* by Khaled Hosseini. Sitting by the shore during a family gathering, being accompanied by that story did not feel like a foreign universe. Reading about war, abuse, and prejudice was not odd for me since I was born under siege in an occupied country, only to witness a war about a year later.

The novel exaggerated the generational trauma that I'd always felt before I could name it. *The Kite Runner* is a narrative of redemption and treachery that everyone should read. It also comments on the war sacrifices, such as Amir escaping to America with his father shortly after the war hit Afghanistan, something I too did. I fled Gaza City, even if unwillingly, for the southern strip.

A matter of minutes separated me and my family from death as the so-called "safe" road leading to the south was bombed just after we passed, killing dozens. That night, guilt washed over me. The same guilt Amir felt for leaving Hassan behind was the same anguish that kept me awake for two nights straight after leaving Gaza City.

I tried hard to find a way to redemption, only to have my hopes dashed by the truth—the truth that many others will be killed and the guilt will never stop growing.

I struggled to accept the truth in lieu of justice while my people were being systematically slaughtered, but eventually, I realized that the truth is not less important than justice. I realized that truth can provide relief, offering a kind of peace. Knowing the truth became important to me, too, and I became ready to give up the right to practice justice in return for hearing or knowing the truth.

I know that the very ending could be interpreted differently by the different people who will experience it, and that is the truth: I want to know how things ended. How did lives end up buried under the suffocating rubble, saturated with the smell of smoke and blood? How did the stories halt mid-sentence?

I hope that recognizing the importance of truth will give birth to a form of hope for both the future of Gazans and perhaps for war-torn Gaza as well.

> When you kill a man, you steal a life. You steal his wife's right to a husband, rob his children of a father. When you tell a lie, you steal someone's right to the truth. When you cheat, you steal the right to fairness.
>
> — Khaled Hosseini, *The Kite Runner*

Lastly, what I truly want is for this era of Gaza to be more than a few rare images on a random website. I want you, the reader, to contribute to preserving the memory of our present and our past. No one wants their home to become a distant, obscure image viewed by strangers in some distant century.

We forget people. After three generations, no one will be remembered. As soon as our memory extinguishes and our name becomes obscure, someone is reminded of a vague memory, and then no one knows that we lived. It's unsettling to think that our lives might be reduced to vague recollections. Despite our yearning to live fully, we must confront the reality that we will eventually be forgotten. We live by this principle, but also ask to be seen as more than just numbers.

We forget people and the core of ourselves. We forget places, and by then, the memories they hold. This is, perhaps, the homesickness we carry not just for Gaza, but for the version of ourselves that once lived there.

Nostalgia may be the only home we have.

Pack up your feed with our past and present. Keep us alive.

Perhaps this is not an introduction, but it is the only way I know how to keep Gaza alive. Because I genuinely want memory to be one of the things that survives, as I can't guarantee my own, and because nothing feels finished. I am still living it... But here, take what I've managed to hold on to.

— Yara & Tareq

OUR WORLD, ALMOST

GAZA, A DIFFERENT TALE

Gaza has always been stereotyped, even demonized. Watching Gaza on the news, one feels it is a battlefield. It is a land of horror and fear. Well, it is true, I have encountered seven hostilities in Gaza since I was born and was notably horrified by the latest protracted war. We have lived a life despite all odds. You may think you know Gaza. But our day-to-day life was always much different from the news. The memories of Gaza are getting heavier now. I have never imagined that we would lose the beauty, simplicity, and spontaneity of the people. I did not imagine that all this would vanish. I could not go forward with my writing without exposing the true Gaza, the Gaza I grew up in, the Gaza I will carry with me, no matter where I go.

I used to accompany my dad, pumping him with my curiosity about Gaza. Did you know that Napoleon stayed in Gaza? He told me once, while I was gazing at the beauty of Al Basha Palace, a historical site that is several hundred years old. It was there, speaking about the deep history of Gaza.

You cannot miss the grand Omari Mosque while in the old city. Always fascinated by its architecture. The Mosque also tells a long history of the different civilizations that crossed Gaza for thousands of years.

The tiny Strip, by the Mediterranean, is quite similar in space to the urban area of Montreal, Canada. Small, yes. But it holds the weight of a world. Highly populated with over two million people, but with so many kind people, living together like a big family. Two-thirds of Gaza's population are refugees, living in eight camps distributed all over the strip. That's a great source of its beauty; those people were displaced from the villages of historical Palestine to the Gaza Strip after the 1948 Nakba, bringing with them a rich, harmonic culture and history.

Gaza City is only the heart, but the magic is there from Beit Hanoun in the far north to Rafah at the very edge of the south. Beit Hanoun is known for its citrus trees. along with its closest rural area of Beit Lahia, are among the most fertile lands. Beit Lahia was once renowned for its strawberries, earning it the nickname "Gaza strawberry," which was exported to various countries. Then comes Jabalia, the famous, highly populated refugee camp—a place always full of life and kindness. Gaza City sits in the center like a heart, with the old Gaza city, a few neighborhoods and the Beach Camp, where, despite 77 years gone of Al Nakba, people there, like all refugees, have not fully established their lives; they still hold the dream of return to their original villages.

Moving south, Nuseirat Camp is renowned for its vibrant markets and a unique blend of traditional and modern shops. Bureij and Maghazi refugee camps are quieter, smaller camps, with families who have lived there for generations, many from villages lost in 1948. Then comes Deir Al-Balah, with its warm people, named after its date palms, which is a peaceful city near the sea.

Khan Younis is a vibrant and bustling city, known for its strong families and large souk. It is also home to the Khan Younis refugee camp, which is one of the largest. And finally, Rafah, right at the border with Egypt. Our gateway to the world. Rafah always felt like waiting, like something was about to happen. It was home to Gaza's only airport, once. And now, it holds the last door to the outside world.

Every area has its unique people, smells, sounds, and memories.

I grew up in Gaza City, specifically in the Al-Rimal neighborhood. It was one of the calmest, most central areas. Clean streets, busy cafes and big supermarkets, several bakeries, and beautiful trees. It was a place where shop owners were friendly and made you feel like part of a large family.

Still, my favorite is Gaza's charming beach. It was not perfect, but it was everything for us; it stretched wide across the western edge of Gaza, always waiting, always moving. Some days it was quiet, some days it was so loud. We did not need fancy resorts or clean sand to love it; we loved it because it was ours.

The water was not always clean, especially near the city, but if we go far enough past the crowds, toward the southern beaches near Deir Al-Balah and Al-Zawayda, it feels different; the sand is softer, the water cleaner. For us, it was more charming and appealing than the Maldives.

There was also the port near Gaza City. That place, built from the rubble of past wars, had a different soul. Fisheries pulling in their nets at dawn. Little boats lined up—kids selling tea and coffee in tiny cups, calling out for customers. Carts offering grilled corn, either in cut cups with salt and lemon, or whole on the cob, grilled and slightly burnt at the edges. And those little noisy kids are playing with the ride-on cars while listening to outdated songs. It was beautiful, always alive. You just sit and watch.

And there were cafes by the sea too, locally known as "Al-Kornesh". Not the kind you see in Europe, but they had plastic and handmade wooden chairs, old speakers playing old Arabic songs, and the sound of waves just meters away. You could sit there for hours with a friend or a book, or just your thoughts.

And beyond the sea, there were many other small things we never thought we would lose.

There was Abu Al-Soud, where we got the best sweets, warm knafeh, dripping with sweet syrup, or fresh Qatayef in Ramadan from Modokh. Somehow, Abu Al-Soud always had a line, especially on holidays.

There were bookstores hidden between busy streets, places where you could still find novels, old poetry books, and secondhand school supplies. One of my favourite spots was the Samir Mansour and Al-Nasr libraries, quiet and peaceful, offering a welcome respite from the outside world.

There was also the main market in Gaza City, Souk Al-Zawiya. Loud, colorful, full of smells and voices and people shouting prices over crates of tomatoes, olives, and fresh mint. We didn't just shop there; we ran into people we knew, stopped for juice, and maybe even argued over which shop had better deals.

Even the mosques had a special feeling. Like Al-Sayed Hashem, this is the grandfather of Prophet Mohammed, buried in the city. Gaza's name is attributed to Hashem when he drove his stick into the ground, an act known as "ghazza" in Arabic; thus, it's called after Hashem's Ghazza. The halls and the walls of the Hashem Mosque seemed to carry centuries of stories. Kids played in the courtyard. Tourists used to visit. Al-Hasayna mosque was my favorite, as it was located right by the seaport, where I would perform Taraweeh and Eid prayers during Ramadan.

And I cannot forget the smell of fresh falafel from Zahran on a Friday morning, or the grilled chicken and rice from Mahran, or the legendary shawarma from Al-Fahd. These were not just meals. They were part of who we were.

There was the family's bakery, known for its bread and ka'ak. We would pass by in the morning, and the smell alone could stop us. Or Al-Yazji Bakery, where they made those soft cheese sandwiches I called "tamees" since I was a kid. It was my comfort and a fast sandwich whenever I passed by.

There were also big stores, such as Metro and Care4, where we went not just for groceries, but to feel a little more normal. To walk the aisles, joke with a friend, and grab ice cream on the way out. Al-Rimal Street was one of my favourite places to walk. It had everything: shops, banks, pharmacies, falafel stalls, and lights that stayed on even when the power went out everywhere else.

And in the heart of Souk Al-Zawiya, between all the chaos and life, there was the phoenix statue. It stood there like a quiet symbol, and somehow it always felt right. Like Gaza itself: always burning, always rising from the ashes.

Gaza had beauty in the small things.

Life was not easy. But it was full. Full of people who made something out of nothing, every single day. That is the Gaza I want to show you.

The Gaza you do not know is real. And it deserves to be remembered in this way.

— Tareq

AND STILL, WE LIVED

A cage, utterly a cage. Talking about Gaza is quite different from experiencing day-to-day life. Life in Gaza was never easy. Yet, a life, a full life. I have always dreamt of exploring the world, but the nightmares and the complexities of travel made this just a fantasy. It could be only because of this that we have learned to accept the minimal and learned to admire the similarity of life. But that drive for freedom was always there, forcibly hidden under the surface.

Even before the famous October, we had already seen too much. There were hostilities before—short ones, long ones, sudden ones. We knew the sound of drones. We knew the rush to store water and bread. We knew what it meant to live with fear.

But still, we lived.

We did not wait for peace to start living. We learned to build our lives around the silence between bombings. Around the short windows of light before the electricity blackout again. Around each other.

I lived in Rimal, in the center of Gaza City. It was a quiet neighborhood. Our home was not big, but it carried everything that made me feel safe. The same furniture we have had for years. The familiar cracks on the wall. My little desk, where I sat and dreamed about becoming a computer expert one day. It was all simple. But it was mine.

We had a routine, even in the midst of chaos. I woke up to the smell of tea and fresh bread.

On school days, I would walk past the corner shops, the fruit sellers, and the old man who sold balloons. Everyone had something to offer, even if it was just a smile.

At school, my favorite day was Tuesday, football day. The schoolyard turned into our stadium. We played like there were no walls around us. I remember once, we got a little too excited and kicked the ball over the school wall. I ran out to find it and saw it stuck under a random car on the street. I pulled it out, held it like I had found something so precious, and ran back smiling. Just like that, we kept playing like nothing else mattered. After school, I would go home and do my homework when there was electricity. If there were

6

not, I would wait. Or light a candle. Or just guess when it might come back.

Thursdays were for family. We all gathered at my grandmother's house. Cousins, uncles, aunts—sometimes thirty people squeezed into one living room. It was loud. It was crowded. It was perfect. My grandmother told stories. My uncle made jokes. We ate whatever we had, and somehow, there was always enough.

Fridays were for the sea. In Al-Zawayda, I would swim with my siblings for a few hours, when the world felt far away. The beach wasn't always clean, but it was ours. Sometimes, my dad and I would swim out a little farther, just the two of us. That's when he would start talking—about life, about the world, about everything, as if the water unlocked something in both of us.

I also talked with random people swimming nearby—strangers who felt like neighbors in the water. We have floated beside each other, chatting like we have known each other for years.

And whenever a big wave came, we didn't run—we faced it. We stood strong and let it crash against us.

I never liked the feeling of water getting in my nose or ears, so I had a trick. Right before diving in, I would press both hands over my face—covering my ears and pinching my nose—then dive deep. That way, when the wave came, I did not feel the chaos above—just movement. Just peace under the surface, like the world was so far away and quiet.

But Gaza was not just about struggle.

There were weddings in the streets. Music blasting from speakers, kids dancing barefoot. There were simple birthday parties with balloons taped to the wall and homemade cake. Students were graduating, shopkeepers painting new signs, and volunteers cleaning the streets.

Gaza was full of people who did not give up.

My friends were studying hard. Some wanted to be doctors, while others aspired to be engineers. Some were trying to get scholarships to study abroad. I was part of a program teaching kids how to code. We believed in the power of education, even when the world told us we shouldn't dream so big.

There was always uncertainty, always tension. But there was also warmth. Community. Strength.

We did not have everything, but we had each other.

And we made it work.

That was our life before everything changed.

Not perfect. Not peaceful. But full of meaning. Full of heart.

And that version of Gaza—the living, breathing, laughing Gaza—deserves to be remembered.

Because it was not just a place under siege.

It was a home.

And it always will be.

— Tareq

THE SKY HAS ALWAYS BEEN LOUD

In Gaza, the sky is never just the sky. It is something you watch with both wonder and fear. As a kid, I would stare up at it, blue and vast and endless— and then, sometimes, it would scream.

But even in a place like that, childhood finds a way. I had a favorite blue shirt. I had a best friend named Ibrahim. I had a school bag that I was proud of, even when its zipper broke sometimes. I played football at school every Tuesday, which was my best day at school. I met my cousins at my grandmother's house every Thursday. I went to swim every Friday in the Al-Zawayda area. My world was small, but it was full.

Still, we kept living. That is what we do in Gaza—we live around the war. We study through it. We laugh in the gaps between sirens. My friends and I used to count how long the electricity lasted and celebrate when it came back, even for an hour.

But even in all that, I had dreams.

I remember, on a Thursday, I sat with my cousins on my grandmother's floor and looked at the stars at night and imagined places I would never see. Places where the sky was just the sky.

I used to wonder how it would feel to walk under a sky that didn't roar. A sky that didn't flash orange in the middle of the night. A sky that didn't hold drones or smoke or fear. Just clouds. Maybe rain.

But even in Gaza, I believed I would one day feel that kind of sky.

Sometimes, I would tell my little sister stories before bed. I made up cities with magic trees and flying bicycles, where people didn't hide under stairs or check the water tank every day, where no one disappeared, where school wasn't cancelled because the school was bombed.

She would laugh and ask me, "Is this real?"

And I would say, "Not yet."

That was the trick in Gaza. We always said "not yet" instead of "never."

Because hope is the only thing they couldn't bomb.

The sky was loud. It still is.

But even now, somewhere deep inside, I wait for the day it goes quiet.

And when it does, I will look up—not in fear, but in peace.

That day has not come.
But we still dream.
And we still live.

— Tareq

THE BREAKING POINT

THE DAY EVERYTHING CHANGED

Tareq's voice:

It was a school holiday.

I went to bed happy, knowing I could finally sleep in—no alarm, no stress—just a quiet day ahead. My bed was under the window, and that night, I slept comfortably. I remember the softness of the blanket, the peace in the room. It was one of those nights in Gaza where everything felt still.

At 6:30 in the morning, I woke up to strange sounds outside my window. Not explosions. Not sirens. Just an unfamiliar noise—shouts, cars, something unsettled. I sat up slowly, confused. My bed was still warm. My body was rested. But something in the air had changed.

I walked to the living room. My dad was already awake. My siblings were just starting to wake up. We turned on the news, but everything was chaotic. Headlines flying across the screen. Reporters talking fast. And yet... we didn't understand anything. Nothing was clear.

Then came the first explosion.

Then another.

We did not know what was happening. We just knew it was big.

My father looked at me. His voice steady, calm:

"Go quickly to the bakery. Get as much bread as you can."

Because in Gaza, when war starts, people do not wait. They run to get food, water, essentials. The bakeries flood. You act fast, or you get nothing.

I ran.

When I turned the corner and saw the bakery, my jaw dropped.

There were so many people. Too many. More than I would ever see.

Lines stretching out to the street, people packed shoulder to shoulder, all waiting for their turns. Some shouting names. Others are just waiting quietly, eyes glued to their phones or the sky.

While I waited, people started talking.

"What is going on?" I wondered

"Did you hear what the news said?"

"They say it is war again... but nobody knows anything."

It felt like the whole neighborhood was standing there, confused but trying to hold it together. Bread was the excuse—but really, we all just needed something to do.

After what felt like forever, my turn finally came.

The man at the door pointed and said, "Come from under!"

They had not opened the bakery door fully—just lifted the big metal market door halfway to keep people from flooding in, so I crouched down and slipped under.

And that is when I was hit with another surprise:

There was another line inside.

Even inside the bakery, people were waiting again. It was hot, packed, loud. Everyone tenses. But no one was fighting. Everyone just... waited. Because what else could we do?

Eventually, I got the bread and hurried back home.

When I reached our building, my father was standing at the door, waiting.

He saw me with the bread and smiled.

Not a big smile. A small one. The kind that says, "You did good. You made it back. We are okay—for now."

That day was supposed to be slow. A break. A chance to sleep in and maybe eat something sweet.

Instead, it became the day everything flipped.

The window that woke me.

The bakery that felt like a battlefield.

The bread that suddenly mattered more than anything else.

That was the day everything changed.

We thought it would be like other times. A few days. Maybe a few weeks. Maybe, at worst, a couple of months like that war back in 2014, when I was in sixth grade.

But it did not stop.

Yara's voice:

The oppressive weight of the morning bore down upon me as I stepped onto my sister's little balcony. The neighborhood felt vast, though each breath was a laborious endeavor. The garden below, with its entangled Jasmine vines climbing the fence wall, had not lost a leaf. The lilies were too pink to believe anything was going wrong. Overgrown paths and the tiles still warm from yesterday's sun mirrored the pretty chaos within my soul. The distant crash of the waves is always a lament, a reminder of dreams unfulfilled and the inexorable march of fate.

In that moment, the boundaries between hope and despair blurred, leaving me suspended in a state of existential contemplation.

I liked the silence. It wasn't eerie. It was Gaza's quiet, the kind that wraps itself around your limbs. Radios murmured in kitchens. Bread bags swung in boys' hands. Falafel oil hissed behind half-open shutters. Everything was normal in a way only Gaza understands. As if people were rehearsing calm, just in case today stayed ordinary.

I had a chemistry exam that day. I was the only one awake in our house. Soft sunlight pooled on my face; the sky was the soft gray of habit, worn from repetition. I stood there holding my tea, steam curling into the 6 am breeze, not in a hurry to leave my hands. If I close my eyes now, I can hear the waves again - their distant, steady hush folding into the morning peace sounding familiar. The Jasmine tea was still hot in my palms, and I didn't mind that I could hear every sip. It made me feel deliberate, full.

A car horn disturbed me—a sharp, living sound in my hush. I watched Ameer, the first grader from the building across, leave his house in that drowsy way of children who still trust the day. He reached the car and, of course, claimed the front seat. That solemn little victory children fight for. That seat always means they've won.

He opened the door. And the sky tore open.

Something harsher than thunder, more final. The kind of sound that feels like it was never meant to be heard by alive beings. It swallowed the birds. The air was crowded with metal and rupture. For a moment, the world held its breath, and so did I.

I ran to check on my younger sister. She stirred in her sleep, her body moving like something rapidly pulled her toward waking. My heart was already wide awake, bracing something colder than panic.

My parents woke up, and I said صباح الخير, a rare thing for me to say in the morning. As quickly as the sky coiled, we had crossed into a different type of morning. The one from which we do not return.

By then, Ameer wasn't in the car. He stood at their window beside his mother, his small hands on the sill, eyes fixed on the street. Watching. Trying to understand the day he'd just been turned away from.

The driver stood next to his car; the door was still open. His arms hung beside him, useless, his gaze fixed on the seat the boy had almost taken. Something in him seemed hesitant, as if he was waiting for someone to give the day permission to continue. Then he looked up at me, smiling, awkwardly—a crooked, almost embarrassed smile. "No school today," he said. His engine was still on.

Suddenly, the morning breeze became subconsciously suffocating. Serene moments became deceptive. The undercurrents of tension gripping the city are no longer oblivious.

My father turned on the television. Hebrew broadcasts. Trying to make sense of what was happening. I opened Twitter. Froze. Closed it. I texted my cousin to see if the bus had brought her sisters back, then we sent some black sarcasm memes, knowing this time we were over, but there was nothing we could really do. So instead, we laughed.

I was supposed to visit the West Bank that month for a friendly volley-ball match. I was oddly excited to see a checkpoint, walk through those metal cattle cages I'd only seen in pictures. What a thing to long for. To want to witness humiliation from the inside. I wanted to see it for myself, just once, for the very first time. The absurdity of wanting to be caged, just so I could know if people look at each other there, or just at the ground. Not because it was okay, I said it's my absurdity. That plan dissolved without anyone saying it was canceled.

We still hadn't eaten breakfast. Baba stood by the sink, staring at the faucet, then the television. We started a list of the things we might need in the next "few days," attending to stock the kitchen with bread, rice, coffee, cat food, anything that might hold through. Gaza's calendars stopped in October.

Later that morning, my father turned the kitchen counter into his desk. His laptop was open, a charger looped around the fruit bowl, a notebook beside it, pages filled with his careful handwriting. His coffee had gone cold. You could see it from the rim, dried into the ceramic.

The cigarette pack was already open. He only smokes during wars. He didn't explain. He lit one and kept working. The smoke lingered in the air longer than it should have.

By noon, the internet went down. We played "shaddah" quietly, almost ritualistically. The same card game from 2014. We played "Handremi", cards sliding in silence except for my brother bluffing a straight with too much confidence. We never said anything when someone had a hand, the winning layout. It was in the way they'd slowly push their cards to the center, eyes avoiding ours. No need for declarations. Just their thud smirk of victory.

We moved the dining table to the living room across the tiles to face the TV. We slept in the living room, laid bed mattresses on the rug in the middle of the room. The others slept there. My father, my brother, and I took the couches. Flashlight only. Solar energy saved for "later". Whatever that meant.

No one said we were taking shifts, but no one really knew how to sleep for full hours. Every so often, an alert. We would pull down the windows, just so the glass would not shatter inward.

My sister would wake up, and we'd hide the window we just pulled down, so she wouldn't realize that an attack was imminent. This doesn't seem to be normal. I don't know what we were thinking of not waking the rest up—I assume it was because we were too used to it, so someone giving a real reaction often feels like exaggerating. We used to tease my sister for it. Now I find her the only one responding appropriately.

It's absurd how the body insists on continuity.

My father juicing pomegranates, pressing the seeds methodically, juice veining the glass, warding off the day.

Me stepping into the basement garden, picking ripened berries, some mint leaves for tea.

Garage door cracking open, my mother walking in back from the hospital, handing us some store-bought groceries.

The noticing. The silence. The ordinary movements we offer up like prayers to whatever god governs survival.

Reflexing.

Denial... it has the face of routine. It is rinsing mint. It is pouring juice. It is standing in the garden, pretending the soil is just soil.

Nothing more on the first day.

The first night.

After that, it wasn't days anymore. Just one long, endless hour.

Days later, they warned our neighborhood at 3 am. I remember moving a chair, senselessly, not caring to pack. There was dust beneath it.

We fled to my aunt's house. Their street was filled with glass from the night before. Ambulances drove fast, headlights off. A neighbor's door, wide open with no one inside.

Hours later, Israelis started ordering people to evacuate Gaza City and the northern areas. We went back home by 7. Decided not to leave home. Later, a sudden fear stoked my mother; we felt it, at least. The food was still warm when we left the house. I didn't take anything with me. Not the book I hadn't finished. I took nothing, and yet I still feel like I left something behind —something invisible, something that made me, me.

I didn't ask where we were going. I didn't say anything about us leaving. I don't know why. There wasn't a scream inside me. No epic moment. Just... subtraction. Something was being taken. And I couldn't stop it.

It starts with a chair slightly moved out of place, with no time to put it back.

I hadn't enjoyed the sunrise in Deir el Balah.

The scent of jasmine still lingered in my chest, a ghost of mornings past. Watching the sky bruise over houses in hues of amber. The Israelis were bombing the periphery. I watched the explosions from a distance. Lost on how to react.

My home had a view that used to hug me each morning. The wind used to move through my hair. I'd push my glasses up to my head to feel the breeze more fully on my face. I never needed sharpness then; I just needed presence. My other senses loved that.

I now evoke that scene, speaking only of yesterdays. I watched my family sleeping; I do not remember crying. The sun began to rise, and a missile hit a house. I watched it from kilometers away. I didn't really react.

I am still savoring my cup of tea, the warmth seeping into my fingertips, grounding me in a scarcely recognizable present. Anchoring me.

Change had not arrived as a tempest, but as a slow, creeping fog, blurring the edges of my world until I could no longer discern where I ended and the new beginnings began.

Time passed. I know it did. It is still morning, technically. But what begins anymore? The sun rises like it owes us nothing. It did feel like an accumulation.

The first strike hit Khan Younis.

But that's the south.

I am back in Gaza City again.

And you always think the bombs will stay elsewhere, like they respect geography.

But it does not feel like a beginning.

The morning tastes the same for nearly two years: the bread is a little dry, the tea too hot, and dust settles in the sugar jar.

Old people always say we only miss things once they stop working. Taps. Lightbulbs. Fathers.

Outside, someone is laughing. A strange, too-loud laugh. A boy selling cigarettes that aren't his. The free water truck honks until everyone wakes to stand in line. I see a man praying behind a tarp sheet. A woman with a cracked bucket, a trail behind her. She moved forward to the nearest manhole. Delivering shame. Even the flies knew what it was. Someone tied a balloon to a tent pole. "Hope," it said in blue. I wanted to pop it with my teeth.

What they don't tell you is that change looks like waiting for the ceiling to collapse and being surprised when it doesn't. It seems like retrieving a birthday letter from the rubble of your bedroom. It seems that speaking less Arabic is an attempt to seek understanding.

I used to pray in the afternoons, after school, before tea. Now, I only pray when I can't sleep. And I often struggle to sleep most nights.

Everything changed, yes.

It changed when we started calling things "temporary" that we still live in.

Then one day, I found a photo of us from before, and I couldn't remember who we were pretending to be.

I still wait for the light to flicker back in our home. It never does.

— Yara & Tareq

IN THE MIDDLE OF IT ALL

This is a shared chapter between Yara and me. You will hear both of us here, and though we were both inside Gaza when the war began, what followed split our paths. I had to leave Gaza, and Yara is still in Gaza.

Some moments are hers. Some are mine. And some belong to both of us. This is what it means to write from the middle of it all.

We always thought of Gaza as a city by the Mediterranean that remains unyielding in the face of storms, its people known for their magnanimity and pride.

But then, one morning, something completely new happened when the sun came out and the streets were filled with the color of blood. This included people walking in the middle of the streets, tents set up on sidewalks, street fights over trivial matters, skyrocketing prices, assaults on public facilities, and even individuals blocking aid trucks with intentions of looting.

You could almost say it is possible to perceive this sight clearly and practically as if it were an ordinary day.

And yet, although we have never personally experienced Gaza in this light, we continue to think that one may live a decent life the day after the crimes cease.

We also noticed that there was a significance to the stones that were stacked up throughout the strip, particularly in Gaza City, where we were living. It seemed as though they had been put there to clear a path.

In all our years, in our brief seventeen years under blockade, we had never experienced such a thing in Gaza. We had that fantasy that the streets we were walking in were only the start of the streets of the cities Nakba had hidden from us.

Now, more than ever, Gaza is experiencing an all-encompassing sorrow for the lost lives, a sorrow that goes beyond mere tears. Beyond all else, it's a challenge. More like getting those souls back.

And perhaps the most brutal truth was this: the pain that began to destroy our naïve minds was that we, the Gazans, the human refugees, are responsible for finding a roof under which to spend the night, waiting for a fleeting hope that would bring some solution.

Tareq's Voice:

The first week was terrifying. The bombing did not let up. The sky was louder than I had ever heard. Gaza was under fire from every direction.

The days became a blur of explosions, news, and fear.

Then came October 13.

Leaflets fell from the sky. Telling everyone to evacuate. To leave Gaza City and move south.

As if leaving was that simple.

As if leaving meant safety.

But we packed. We had no choice.

I looked at my room one last time. My desk, where I dreamed of being a computer expert. The walls I painted myself. My books, my memories. All of it.

Then I heard my father shout, "We need to leave, now!"

And just like that, we walked out.

We moved to Khan Younis in the south. So did thousands of others—families carrying whatever they could, children crying, elderly people being pushed in wheelchairs. We all thought the South would be safer.

But it was not.

Even schools were hit. Even hospitals. Nowhere felt safe. We saw things I cannot put into words.

We moved again—to Rafah, right near the border. For three long months, we lived in a place that felt like time had stopped. Gaza was collapsing in front of us. Entire cities flattened. Roads gone. Landmarks turned to dust.

I cooked over open fires. I carried water in buckets. Sometimes we used seawater. Sometimes we had nothing. That became normal. I woke up every day trying to figure out how to make it to the next day.

We had no electricity. No gas. No internet. Just darkness. I stopped checking the date. Time no longer mattered.

The sky. The bakery. The road south. The fire. The silence. The loss.

Everything changed.

And yet... somehow... we are still here.

Still standing. Still carrying bread through chaos. Still smiling when we see each other, safe at the door.

Because in Gaza, we do not wait for the storm to stop living.

We live through it.

And that—no matter what—is something no one can take from us.

In the 350-square-kilometre Gaza Strip, there are no places for camping.

There is no desert in the most densely populated area on earth. From Beit Hanoun and Beit Lahia in the north to Rafah in the far south, there is no private recreational space available.

Can displacement ever feel like camping? Not even close. However, being forced to leave our homes with nothing to survive on pushed us to be creative. We made use of coastal areas and abandoned farmland, relying on the most basic survival skills.

In Rafah, a statue of an aircraft stood at the center of a roundabout. "Al Tayara", as in the Arabic language, was a daily destination for us, where we would go to buy food from tens of street vendors randomly occupying the street.

But why an aircraft? I wondered.

Rafah was once home to Arafat International Airport. To me, this was more of a story—something I had never seen myself. However, my dad told me that the airport had indeed existed, inaugurated by U.S. President Bill Clinton in 1998, but completely demolished by Israel in 2001.

Still, what stood out most about Rafah was not just the aircraft in the roundabout. The time in Rafah allowed me to explore the city, despite the huge danger of moving around. My friends and relatives were dispersed in shelters around the city; approximately one million people relocated there, in addition to the 300,000 people who were already living there. I was joining my mom to visit my grandmother, calling my friends to meet at specific points, and going on a daily journey to look for wood, cooking gas, and any food.

In my daily journeys, I felt like flying among countries. Metaphorically, of course.

Our shelter was located near the Swedish Village, a neighborhood in the far south of the Gaza Strip. It was a home village for the fishers of Rafah. The military invasion of Rafah damaged it.

To travel east to Rafah, you would pass landmarks like the Qatari Hospital, a still unfinished hospital, but a friend from Rafah told me that this was a dream to the people there. Rafah never had a proper hospital, and people would often go to either the European Hospital in Khan Younis or Shifa Hospital in Gaza City.

Then, not far from the Qatari Hospital, comes the Saudi Neighborhood, and then the Emirati Quarter. That did not seem like a Gulf-like area at all, but rather housing projects filled with thousands of tents now.

Just beyond the Emirati quarter, you would find the Canada Neighborhood or camp. This is not a new area. It was there for over 70 years. At some point, Canada supported the establishment of a refugee camp.

Further along, one would come across the Kuwaiti Hospital, and then the Brazilian Neighborhood, until finally reaching the "Al Awda" roundabout, which translates to "The Return," symbolizing the Palestinians' right to return following Al-Nakba.

I had never been to Rafah before, this southern city, but I can say that mingling there and meeting people from various parts of the Gaza Strip was an interesting experience. However, people were not planning to stay long. They seemed anxious and worried. Even within the Strip, the urge to go back home was intense. In every conversation I overheard, people spoke with fear, often recalling the trauma of Al Nakba.

It was not a pleasant experience. I, too, began absorbing their fears, sensing that another forced diaspora might be on the horizon, especially as my family started planning to leave Gaza, not by plane, but by crossing into Egypt for a journey into the unknown.

Yara's Voice:

Back home, remnants of the Israeli Army have left a haunting imprint on my home.

Graffiti adorns the walls, bearing evacuation directions, primarily intended for soldiers.

Yet, the marks extend beyond mere drawings; they encompass the wreckage of furniture, the demolition of walls, the smashing of doors and gates, the dismantling of solar panels, and the uprooting of every flower and ornamental plant.

In the wake of such devastation, we find ourselves voiceless, unable to lament our losses—be they the homes reduced to rubble or the loved ones we mourn.

The irony is starkly evident in the location chosen for the "LOL Israel" mark, situated near our plastic swimming pool—a symbol of innocence and recreation that was full of water and used just days prior to the conflict.

There was no hint of "extremism" within our home, no incitement to violence. And believe me when I say a house with a hint of "extremism" does not exist in Gaza. Even the flowers, once proudly displayed by the door, were callously uprooted.

Pondering the rationale behind the army's actions yields no solace, nor does it answer our myriad questions. Who, indeed, cares for our inquiries and our anguish?

Witnessing Israeli soldiers brazenly parade items pillaged from Gaza homes, we are met not with remorse but with indifference.

Examining the photos sent by our neighbors, my dad noticed the absence of our cherished family albums. Even this aspect of our existence, like so much of Palestinian life, fades into the realm of oral history.

Every flower in our home was familiar to us—the hues, the fragrances, even the subtle signs of health or a need for vitamins. Each morning, there was a ritual stroll, bidding good day to the blossoms. We poured our hearts into creating what we believed to be our dream abode, relishing the company of visitors who graced our threshold.

I can hear the walls begging us, asking when we will return. I want to scream back:

Not all who left have vanished, and not all who stayed have remained.

I did not think I would return.

I did not think there would be a road back.

I did not think I would walk it.

But I did. Twice.

And now I live in what remains.

We were only allowed to return after they received their settler.

I keep thinking of how one settler can disturb the rights of a home from a million people. I keep thinking about how angry I was when we had to delay walking to Gaza, just because they did not allow that.

I must confirm that I sometimes lost hope of coming back, but I now cannot name a moment I was happier than the moment I took my first step on the way back home.

I did not sleep well that night; I just kept thinking about how our home now looked, how the Israelis had treated it throughout the days.

I was just waiting for the moment they would leave it, because it was our time to return.

On our way to Gaza City, my dad took tens of pictures and videos. That is when I knew that part of what he had lost was coming back.

I watched his gaze all along the way home.

I promised myself not to cry, even though we did not know if it was still there or not.

We reached the path leading to our home. That's when I took a deep breath.

I heard everyone holding their breath.

Then I opened my camera again and continued to film everything, since my mother, little sister, and brother couldn't join us, as we had just gone there to check.

We could not help it; we walked twenty-five kilometres that day.

You know, nostalgia can kill.

I started pointing out the neighbours' houses, the building we lived in for two years, which was bombed two days after this catastrophe started—and it was my first time seeing it in ruins.

Then I was a few steps away from my actual home.

I tried to fight my tears. I tried my best, but I couldn't help but cry.

I wanted, in that moment, to ask our home for forgiveness—for leaving it behind in the name of fake safety.

It felt as if the colors had been drained out of the whole neighbourhood.

It is a nightmare I have seen many times before, right in front of me, but not as something fictional.

It is my neighborhood.

That is the part I never imagined writing.

Everything felt out of place.

Even me.

It was too quiet.

I expected relief.

Perhaps I got something else—a tightness in my chest, like home was waiting to ask me where I had been.

And that is when I remembered the nightmare, one I have seen even when awake.

Now, standing here, I could not tell if I was dreaming again or if the dream had been waiting for me all along.

In that dream, I could not bear to look back. I was scared to think back on the day I left Gaza. If I stopped to think about it, all I could see was a flash that would not give me time to hear the explosions. All I shall experience is my feet's reluctance to go into the unknown and into a place where I have no home. You cannot always laugh when you live here. I just had a deep affection for Gaza, though.

The houses that exist now, if any, and the streets appear to be getting smaller by the second. The souls that flood the sky and the severed limbs that are still yearning for their owners cause drones and pilots to stumble. I think the sound of the resurrection is comparable to that of an aircraft. Waking the dead every day from their never-ending slumber. I look everywhere for a sky that is devoid of death. I am positive it is there when I check the alleyways and streets. It is claimed that justice exists beneath that sky. Justice is what I have always yearned for and pursued.

Day by day, my inquiry grew until I came upon a road that was dark and covered in reddish-brown dust. It represented the path between one war and another with a slightly destroyed-looking home at its end. I noticed a glistening light out in the distance. I certainly lost my mind. When there is no flame to ignite a cigarette, how can someone even light a candle? My head was heaving. My vision has become blurry. All night long, I waited there. The light was growing more luminous. I followed my feet to the front door of the residence. This could be hell.

The light continued to lead me farther into the house until I entered what appeared to be a living room. It was extremely cold, and there was a strong, unpleasant smell that seemed like blood. When I looked up at the ceiling, I realized that I was staring at the sky, which appeared to be a mirror reflecting everything I had not experienced in this room. There were muttering noises coming from the corner that sounded like greetings. I then raised my gaze once more to the sky. To discover that I was surrounded by freshly bloodied corpses. The murmuring then stopped, and the light gradually faded out.

Regarding the sky, I felt as though it was falling. How in the world could the sky fall? Although I almost carried myself, I wanted to carry the sky. My breathing became more labored as the room seemed to shrink. There were mutters all around, but this time they were more audible. I felt like ghosts were begging me to flee from the start. There was no way out then but death. How am I supposed to play a game with fate? I have not yet met my demise.

I was sprinting toward the door when I last remembered anything. I needed to find a way out. Everything in my immediate vicinity disappeared. Then, from somewhere in the shadows farther down the hallway, came the cry, "You can never leave." The entire house trembled. Something that sounded like a rocket caught my attention. A rocket descended to end my fate.

I was still in the place where my family and I had been relocated when I opened my eyes. It was a bad dream.

And only then, standing in front of my home a year and a half later, did I realise that the house from the nightmare was my actual home.

Nevertheless, every night I hear the same muttering. Death is the only way out of this place. Still unanswered is my question: where is that sky, and why couldn't the sun drive out the darkness? The sun doesn't remain; why is that?

Forgive me for entwining you in this tragic narrative before extending an invitation to a home that now lies in ruins, unfinished, and forsaken.

Nostalgia is a disease, and time can never return.

After containing my tears, I intended to step inside. My mind ran ahead of my body, wearing my fear of what I would find. I could already smell the rotten food from the kitchens, notice things that weren't ours, and see the stained blood on a doorframe.

Then I searched for my dad. I genuinely wanted to see his reaction. I saw him standing—just standing there with his hands on his waist—staring.

My sister and I went inside immediately, running between rooms to seek anything left of our belongings. I looked for any of mine. I had piles of unread books, and more piles of books I loved.

Then I looked again for my dad and saw him still standing in front of our home, staring. He did not seem to be bothered by the sunlight on his face. It is one of those times when I struggle to find the right words to describe the look on his face. He looked like he was lost in a labyrinth of not knowing why all of this happened in the first place—and even relieved, because, yeah, at least the home is still there.

I heard him telling one of his friends that we did not dare to hope it would be there. Because, when almost the whole neighborhood was carpet-bombed, one feels shame for having their house at least still standing.

It is kind of unsettling when I look again at one of his writings, where he said:

In the unfortunate event of our demise, we are open to a mass grave, expressing our love for each other. If burial is not possible, a tombstone with the words 'six innocent souls, lived and lay here' near our home would suffice, adorned with red roses, a favorite of our daughters.

Then I see him standing, staring at his home, grateful just because it exists. Or maybe because we still have our tombstone there.

Ultimately, I went to check the rooftop, also to gain a clearer view of the entire neighborhood. A wave escaped the sea, and I felt as if it hit me in the face. Scowling birds were flying; their feathers were dry. They reminded me of our bird—the one we accidentally forgot in the house. I keep imagining what that bird witnessed, but I keep those wonders to myself. People who lost their families won't bear me talking about a bird. And I get that.

I used to think my neighborhood was one of the calmest in the city. Now it's funny how, when I tell anyone I used to live there, all they can say is: "Oh, I see why you are not living there anymore." Even my mother called it a desolate neighborhood. This place now creates death. My house is a heap of scattered stories. My dreams are broken under its missing door. My heart hears the silence's voice.

I couldn't find the right words to describe the inside of the house, or even my own room. And I feel odd that I can't accept the truth. I can't accept that this is our home now, but I just can't bring myself to say it out loud. Maybe that is why I can only write it down.

But something about our home still hangs on with hope: our little berry tree is still alive, roses are still blooming, and one of our wooden swings is still swinging—calling for us to come and live there again.

On our way back to Deir al-Balah, where we evacuated, the scene was still the same as in the morning: people pulling piles of everything they'd managed to hold onto throughout the sixteen months of displacement; children carrying empty gas cylinders; fathers and sons pushing—and sometimes carrying—their parents and kids.

Anyone with a mind can admit that most people had no idea how far they would need to walk. Everyone thought it would be one of those short strolls along the promenade—an hour-long walk at most. However, what made it worse is that, at the very least, someone responsible should have treated people with the care they deserved, starting with something as basic as ensuring they had access to water on the road. Or maybe preparing the path people walked on.

I remember that day: we had to walk over three or four earthworks, cross big holes—sometimes walking on wrecked wood, sometimes on nothing at all— not to mention the sewage that filled up the streets.

Walking against the crowd, people thought we were crazy. Because when everyone else was dying to reach the city that day, we decided to walk that road twice, with real minds in our heads. I remember sharing the last bottle of water with a little boy on the road, providing first aid to a woman who had collapsed, and insisting that we not stop walking, so our legs wouldn't hurt more.

I intended to write about some of the details of the road leading to the city, to show the side the media ignored. Again, they adopt the narrative where Gazans are superheroes—people who walk kilometres knowing their homes are no longer there—without taking the time to talk about how this road added to the offence of what's left of Gazan dignity.

I am not very sorry to say that the media is drowning in hypocrisy.

And not being the kind of person who only talks about the sort of pain that makes us question whether anyone truly cares about our very human rights, I will add this: along the way, I saw bittersweet moments. Lovers and friends hugging, finally reunited. They can now mourn together. Cry together.

— Yara & Tareq

I DID NOT SAY GOODBYE

I did not say goodbye.

Not because I forgot. Not because I was in a rush. But because I could not.

How do you say goodbye to a place that raised you? To a life you did not finish living?

People talk about closure, about saying goodbye properly, about getting that moment to say thank you, to cry, write a letter, or hold a childhood memory one last time. But sometimes life does not give us that kind of goodbye. Sometimes, goodbye is quiet. Sometimes it is in the way we do not look back because we know if we do, we will not move forward.

Perhaps part of me thought that if I didn't say goodbye, then this wasn't goodbye.

One day, the door would still be there, and our table would still have a seat with my name. That Gaza would still know me.

Maybe one day I will get the chance to return. Perhaps I will stand in front of that door again and finally let the words out.

And maybe that is my way of keeping Gaza with me.

But even if I did not say goodbye, I still remember everything.

So, no. I did not say goodbye.

But I carried it all with me. Every corner, every voice, every unfinished day.

Gaza is still with me. In how I speak. In how I dream.

Even in exile, I am still of that place.

And that is something no border can take from me.

Below is a message I wrote while crossing the border that day. I did not edit it. I did not change a word. It was just me, in that moment:

February 25, 2024 – 11:37 AM

Day 140 of the war in Gaza

I am writing these words while passing the border from Gaza toward Egypt, along with my mother and three siblings.

What is to come is entirely unknown. I feel stressed, fearful, and anxious about what is ahead.

28

But I know this is a turning point in my life—and in my family's. A big jump in this journey. We are still holding onto hope. Hope for a brighter future.

I am writing this message because I know I will keep reading it in every chapter of my life. I will read it with a smile. A smile that holds both pain and pride—pain for what we left behind, our beloved Gaza, and pride that I endured. That I kept going. That I kept facing life, no matter how hard a chapter of it became.

I want my heart back, my beloved Gaza.

Even though I've left, my heart is still there. It refuses to accept any new home. We once had 365 square kilometers of home, and 2.3 million family members. Now we are alone. We have left it all behind—for strangers, for the unknown.

However, I am 100% certain that better days are ahead. A brighter future is waiting. And I will reach the place I have always dreamed of.

— Tareq

FIRST STEP IN DIASPORA

We had been moving for weeks. From Gaza City to Khan Younis. From Khan Younis to Rafah. To anywhere that had not been bombed yet.

At first, we told ourselves this was temporary. That we would go back once the fire settled. Like we always did.

But something about this war felt different. More final. More suffocating. Like Gaza was collapsing from the inside out, and we were just waiting to be buried next. In Rafah, we lived in borrowed time and borrowed space. Every day came with new losses. Food, water, homes, people. There was nothing left to pretend with. We were no longer surviving. We were dissolving.

Some people we knew started leaving Gaza, and this is when we started thinking about it.

Could we leave?

Should we?

Who gets to choose exile while others are buried under it?

Do we die with it, or walk away with what is left?

One night, it became clear – we could not stay. We had run out of waiting. That is when the decision was made. Quietly. Almost reluctantly. Like breathing underwater. We would leave.

I would describe it more that Gaza was pulled out of us piece by piece, rather than that we just left. And maybe that is what broke me most as we were raised to resist, to stay, to cling to land and memory.

Suddenly, on the night of February 24, 2024, our names were on the lists—a permission slip to exile. I did not feel lucky. I felt gutted, as if it were a wound.

And that is where the story of diaspora begins.

We woke up the next day at 6am, packed our bags, and crossed the border. I left with my mother and three younger siblings. My father stayed behind as he was needed for his work with humanitarian work with the people. I remember the moment we said goodbye; it did not feel real. We just held on for a few seconds, then let go.

Stepping into Egypt felt different, as if we had just entered a new, separate world. The roads are wide, the buildings untouched. But nothing about that felt comforting; it just felt unreal. I would describe it as if we were walking in a dream, where everything looked normal, but nothing made sense.

I kept thinking, what now? We had crossed and were now safe. I realized that safety is not peace, not belonging, not home. We were not going back tomorrow. Or next week. Or maybe ever.

And this was the first step in diaspora, when we realized we had nowhere to return to and nowhere to land.

The days that followed were slow and strange. No airstrikes. No sounds of drones. No rush to store water or food. But inside, I was wired for it all. I remember being scared of the regular airplane sounds, especially when landing and departing from Cairo's airport.

In the quiet of those early days, I began to understand what the term 'diaspora' truly meant.

At first, I thought that meant safety. But very quickly, I realized it meant something else: uncertainty. That fear of not knowing what is next. We were not home anymore. And we were not settled anywhere either. We were something in between. Where do we go? What do we do? Who are we now?

We tried to build routines. Wake up. Eat something. Scroll through the news. Try to understand where we were, and what this new life was asking of us. There were some tasks. Paperwork. Embassies. Long lines. The endless waiting that comes with being displaced. We are constantly proving who we are to people who will never really understand what that means—carrying documents that try to summarize a life, explaining things that do not fit into forms.

The hardest part was pretending we were okay, so the others would not worry. And yet somehow, we kept moving. Not because we were strong, but because there was no other choice.

And so, this is how it began, with a goodbye that did not feel finished. A step we did not want to take. A path life has forced on us.

I do not know what comes next.

But I know this was only the first step.

And I am still walking.

— Tareq

WHAT WILL TOMORROW LOOK LIKE?

I don't know what tomorrow will bring.

But I know it must come.

Maybe not quickly. Maybe not easily. But someday, somehow—it will.

And when it does, I want to be ready for it. I do not want to show up tomorrow as just a person who survived. I want to show up as someone who tried to do something with all this pain. Someone who carried the weight but did not let it bury him.

Because if we have made it this far, we owe it to ourselves—and to those who did not—to try.

I do not imagine tomorrow as perfect. It will not erase what happened. It will not bring back the people we lost or fix everything we are carrying now. But I imagine a day when we can finally breathe. Where we do not feel like strangers everywhere we go.

I want a tomorrow where Gaza is not just in headlines. Except in cases where it is reduced to rubble or a war zone. I want a tomorrow where people talk about Gaza and think of resilience, creativity, beauty—because that is the Gaza I knew. That is the Gaza I carry with me.

I want people to remember that even during the worst moments, we still managed to live. We still made jokes. We still helped each other. We still believed in tomorrow, even when we didn't know if we'd make it through the night.

I want a future where my little siblings grow up with memories that do not include bombs. Where schools are for learning, not sheltering. Where we stop having to learn how to run, how to hide, how to say goodbye too early.

I do not want their dreams to be shaped by fear. I want them to grow up dreaming freely—about art, science, building things, travelling, just simply living.

That is what I want to hold tomorrow.

And honestly, I want a tomorrow where I don't have to keep explaining who I am, where I'm from, or why I left. I want a tomorrow where I can say "I am from Gaza" and not feel like I need to add context, or watch people shift uncomfortably, or turn me into a sad story.

I am not a tragedy. I am a person.

I am someone who had to leave home, but never left it behind.

In the future, I hope my father will be with us again. We are sitting around the same table. No signal issues. No updates from the daily war. Just us. As a whole family. Not half here, half there.

In that version of tomorrow, we are not wondering what to do next. We are building. We are working. We are helping others stand back up, too.

That is what keeps me going.

I know that maybe tomorrow will not come soon. And perhaps it will not come the way we expect. But we are already shaping it, every day. With every story we tell, every time we show up for each other, every time we hold onto dignity in a world that tries to strip it away, we are building tomorrow.

And I want it to be one we are proud of.

Not a perfect one. But one that is ours.

We did not choose this path. We did not ask for exile. For war. For separation. But we are here. And now it is up to us what we do with that.

So, I will keep imagining tomorrow.

I will keep walking toward it, even if it is far.

Because maybe, in all this loss, there is still a chance to create something new.

Not to replace what was taken.

But to honor it.

To carry it forward.

And to say, in our way:

We are still here.

And we are not done yet.

— Tareq

REFLECTIONS

SHOULDERS MUST REMAIN STRONG

In Palestinian culture, we are raised on the proverb *My shoulders are your subsistence and supply; my tears are your water.* The best English translation would be "lean on me when you are not strong." We, Palestinians, have practised this proverb our whole lives, and we have concluded that giving is a greater feeling than receiving.

We have always shown solidarity with an open heart, demonstrating love, smiles, and resilience. Over the years, this method has been successful; we've shared in people's struggles and pain. This affirms that Palestinians are accustomed to supporting all suffering people worldwide, empathising with their pain as it mirrors their own. Today, with every breath, we must deal with the fact that our hearts are injured, severely injured, and the possibility that we may no longer be able to give is getting closer and closer.

The smell of death lingers and sticks to our clothes. We cannot simply avoid it. Before death comes, we need to make sure that our shoulders are strong enough to carry more than just subsistence; we, especially Gazans, have to carry more than is possible. We need to ensure that we can give and not wait to receive. Some will leave suddenly, and some will remain on their shoulders until the moment they fall apart. For those who wish to pour out their stress, anger, frustration, and pain, please give them the address of our graves. Tell them we will be listening and crying for their pain. Just don't look towards our hearts.

— Yara

THE OTHER DEATH

I find it funny how most of the titles I include are inspired by typical moments in my daily life. Here, you spend your day revising your lifetime and the months spent on nothing, no matter what you're doing.

I was hesitant to write what follows. Vulnerability always felt heavy, because, tragically, I don't place much worth on what might seem like a problem to people who live more peaceful lives, because I just can't bear the comparison to what my people are living through.

But then I realized that sharing this might set a form of understanding for what I call "survivor's guilt".

And because I must share raw experiences from my perspective, not just reflections on emotions that may seem vague to some.

After evacuating Rafah, I initially had trouble sleeping. On a personal level, my body can't adapt quickly if I change my pillow, so imagine evacuating, once again, from a place that wasn't home in the first place. Getting used to a new house that isn't yours, to streets you know nothing about, isn't that kind of an easy task.

Summer came, and I still couldn't sleep with ease, but at least I caught a few hours when my mind surrendered to the silence.

My brother used to work as a translator with a medical organization, trying to keep up with his medical studies. Their work was tough, and he isn't the kind of person who talks about his day. But out of the ordinary, one day he told us about a young woman who had drowned in the sea while taking a bath. She died, just like that.

We always had the feeling that the sea is a boundary, and the sole escape from the confines of our existence.

For years, it remained the only sanctuary for us. Yet, as "the ugly ducklings", we found ourselves condemned to an inescapable fate. The sea, which is somehow a solace, also harbors peril. Its promise of a refuge can swiftly turn into a tragedy.

Later, we found out the young lady was the daughter-in-law of a man I find very inspiring. And, in one of those blatant ironies Gaza is full of, Israeli Forces imprisoned her husband. And as many of the stories in this place end, the mother died and left her two-year-old daughter to face the unvarnished truth. The one that lays bare the cruelty of pigs on the wing.

The day passed, and a kind of hunger strike followed my disturbed sleep. My body refused food for days. I remember that the food at the time was better than it had been many times before. And this led me to think that this was the problem. I could not bear the fact that we could afford what others couldn't. I couldn't overcome that what was "bothering" me was still incomparable to what they were subjected to.

Or maybe it was a desperate attempt to escape. That's when my body collapsed over, and over, as if it were trying to alert me, one that I shouldn't fail my family, or maybe a sign that this was not the right way to stand for them.

I remember that was when we paused working on the book. I was in a place where I was questioning my very existence.

During the healing process, my family and I would take the car and drive to the closest point to our home. Though home was still kilometers away, it was my absolute favorite spot. I knew it might make things heavier, given that I was being forced into diaspora. But it gave me a few minutes away from the noise of displacement. That street was full of tents. Maybe I was fighting my noise, to find peace standing on the edge of the only place I know. Still wanting to capture the sunset, even though a warship at sea might shoot me down.

My father and I also had a daily ritual: we would walk along the beach until we reached the same point, about nine kilometers away.

We just walked. The displaced, living in tents, had come to rely on the sea for their most basic needs. That reliance underscores a stark fact that even they know, deep down, that our attempts to coexist may, paradoxically, lead to our undoing.

I still have days when my body feels like it's crumbling. However, I have now started to approach it differently, as if I had to shift the way I perceive things. To throw away some of what I carry on my shoulders. Not out of selfishness, but because what I feel is also worth a stand from me. To still have something to fight with.

Sometimes, I feel like it's a sign. To do nothing but keep swimming, with nothing really on my mind.

All I know is that I have to talk this stress out. To find that missing part of the puzzle.

Maybe I won't find it today. Perhaps I won't understand it. Maybe it's not what I want. But I feel closer than ever. More real than I've ever been before.

On the edge of yesterday,
On the edge of tomorrow,
Just not today.

"Here and now" is a lie I tell myself.

We are what we were during this fight. And we can't neglect the truth that if we don't hold ourselves accountable, how can we expect anyone else to take a step toward our justice?

When some stole the starving's right to food, how can we expect others to care about our hunger?

These are not words meant to satisfy those involved in our slow, systematic killing. These are not justifications. This is agony, for their failure to build a human being who would give up their ego and greed, just to keep whoever is left alive. It's for their inability to heal the shattered, their failure to restore what can never be reclaimed. Human dignity.

This is a moment where I can finally try to put it all together. We unravel the loss of ourselves... of something sacred... our very humanity.

Maybe, at first, my naive self didn't know that minimizing my pain would only make it worse.

And by understanding its worth, I can finally stand up for the pain of others.

— Yara

ONLY THE SMOKE MOVED

I sat down and told her:
You left me confused.
She said nothing.
Only the smoke moved.

I added:
I saw the sea again today.
It was calm.
The kind of calm that makes you nervous.
But I kept running to it.
Do you not know I walked over ash just to remember your name?
But after the second tent was torn.
The waves forgot how to lull.
Who taught you to make martyrs out of morning light?
Then bury them along with the sunset?

That's when my prison became crystal clear.
That's where the bodies go.
The sea's beautiful.
But it carries too many to be innocent.

What do I do with all the graves inside my throat?

She said:
Go away

And I said:
But I'm the dust that clings to your door

She wondered:
What door?
I laughed, then I said:
The one who'll wash that dust away one day.
The sea will wash me away.
Will wash us all away.

She said:
That's not strange.
That's just what I've turned you into.
Dust.

I didn't like that. I told her so.

I said:
You've made it easier to witness a massacre than missing someone.
Easier to expect loss than imagine a future.
Easier to escape home.

She asked:
What do you want from me?

I said:
I want to stop writing about you to fill my emptiness.
I want to miss you for your silence.
I want you to be boring again.
That background noise.
Where you don't have to be everything.

She looked at me then.
For real.
And said:
I want that too.
Then she added:
You know I've never been gentle.
Why do you keep expecting me to change?

GAZA HELD IN TIME

I said:
Because I hated surviving,
the moment you lost your temporary silence.

She said:
That version is gone.

I said:
No.
They buried her in us.
And we carry her around like a second spine.
Digging her up ever since.

She said:
You really think memory is enough?

I said:
It's all I have, and I hate it.

Then I went quiet
Because how do you argue with someone who's been gone?

She asked:
Are you afraid of losing me?

And I said:
I'm afraid you'll keep surviving this way.

Survive just enough,
for the world to forget you're dying.
I'm afraid we'll survive too well,
and call it life.

She said nothing.
She didn't flinch.
She never does.
Only the smoke moved.

— Yara

THE TAROT LADY SAYS
LIFE OWES US AN APOLOGY

I wander the city
Desperately
careful not to meet anyone's eyes
not out of shame, but fear that a second too long
Would make them feel exposed...
Seen.
as if I'd caught sight of their open wounds, as if I'd stepped into their tents,
heard their arguments. Uninvited.
Unwilling. But not untouched.
I carry the tears
of a mother crying silently, the quiet prayers of a father begging for his
    own child's safety.
Praying...
To find a way out of here,
because this place
is no longer the one we knew.

Here...
One must walk with one truth in mind:
Maybe other people in the street
are carrying something heavier.
And even if they don't you must believe they might.
You must overlook your ego
And let that belief soften the edge of our stolen empathy.

Everyone
Is fighting in a battle
they cannot name nor escape.

Tell me,
What could drive
a girl my age
to lean against the ruins
of a bombed-out car,
shaking,
bursting with tears
as if something sacred was lost?
But an open wound.

I wanted to go to her. To sit there. Say nothing. Just share the silence.
    I wanted to be courageous enough... to break, too.
To fall apart beside her.
    To let her know she isn't the only one grieving in plain sight.
But that fear returned the same fear of seeing... and being seen.

Because maybe she needed the aloneness. Maybe that, too, was sacred.

We do everything alone here. We walk alone through a battle
    that has no ending nor a beginning...

Still, I wish she could know I felt her. She isn't alone.
That this may seem quite relatable
Maybe these words could be a refuge for someone else, too
someone who thinks they're the only one broken.
Call it a solace.
But I...
I am a coward,
Who's filled with emptiness,
hollowed,
afraid,
holding too much,
offering too little.
Carrying her deep into my heart
Silently.

— Yara

A CEMETERY WITH MOVING BODIES

One of the most dangerous consequences of the genocidal war in Gaza is the destruction of human dignity. And it's a daily, deliberate reality. You feel it most in the eyes of those who used to stand tall. People who, just months ago, ran shops, clinics, schools—people who never imagined they'd be reduced to chasing trucks for a sack of flour or begging for a tent to shield their children from cold and fire.

There is no healing without justice, no justice without naming the crime.

Dignity collapses quietly first: when the house falls, when the bakery vanishes, when you can't find clean water. But it shatters loudly when your child asks what they did wrong to deserve this life. The Gaza economy has always been fragile, fragile by design, but now, even that frailty has been bombed out of existence. There is no "middle class" anymore, only those still crawling out of rubble, and those buried beneath it.

We know the war is not over. The missiles still scream. Yet already, we're being told to survive on rations, to wait for aid that might never come. We are being forced into a life of professional begging. Not by nature. By policy. A life dependent on donations is not a life, it's managed starvation with polite packaging. Even during a crisis, aid is meant to support.

Aid distribution is normal and necessary during and post crisis, while dependence on aid for extended periods is a crisis in itself.

But when aid becomes the only structure left standing, it is not relief, it is a slow erasure.

We are living through the collapse of everything that made life human.

Even our pain is censored. Even our resistance is criminalized.

And no one can tell us what happens next.

The world negotiates our survival in exchange for our silence.

Will we sleep in tents for years? Will children grow up between nylon walls, learning to draw with ash? What happens when the world moves on —again—and the only ones left to remember this horror are the ones who couldn't escape it?

We will not wake up to our city as it was, nor escape from the nightmare of destruction we're still living.

Whoever dares to govern Gaza after this must face a broken people. And that governance must begin with rejecting the systemic dependency being designed for us. Rebuilding can't mean handing out bandages. It must mean restoring the ability to live without asking for permission.

But to do that, the world must decide—right now—what it wants. Will you let Israel kill us all? Is that the plan? Or will someone finally step up and demand that we be given the minimum requirements for a dignified life?

And for those cheering the destruction, remember this:

Tanks and warplanes don't feed seagulls.

What they do is feed the earth with bones. And the earth is full.

Gaza today is not a city. It is a cemetery with moving bodies. A place where over 50,000 people have been killed. Where thousands more remain trapped under collapsed buildings. Where people build shelters from garbage and cook over wood while new bombs fall. There are no words for the stench of bodies. No words for the parents digging through rubble with their hands, hoping to find a piece of their child they can still recognize.

People talk of resistance as if it were a choice. But when your life is made unlivable, resistance is breathing. It is holding your baby close and refusing to surrender them to silence. It is refusing to apologize for surviving.

If your goal is to eliminate us, then be honest. Drop the final bomb. Get it over with. At least let us hug our children before the blast. Do not dress it up in false concern, in humanitarian pauses, in slogans about peace.

We have heard it all before.

We are not allowed to mourn. We are not allowed to speak. We are barely allowed to exist.

Even in death, we are dehumanized. Accused of being numbers. Of being in the way.

Well, then, have the decency to bury us when you're done.

Because our bones still carry dignity.

We live in a world of sacred lies. A world where the word "human" is only granted to some. Where massacres are livestreamed, and the algorithm scrolls past.

So, let us say it plainly:

Not all lives are equal in this world.

Not all suffering is acknowledged.

Not all deaths are mourned.

Some nations allow it to be committed under the banner of self-defence. There are children whose deaths are explained away. There are hospitals bombed with impunity. There are prayers turned into targets.

And Palestinians are expected to thank the world for its silence.

No. We will not thank you.

We will not forgive you.

Our blood is not a bargaining chip.

We are not asking for charity. We are asking for justice. For the right to grieve openly, to live without apology. For the world to stop pretending it doesn't see what's being done.

If the system can't treat us as humans, then it is the system that must be abolished.

And still, despite all of this, we still somehow resist humiliation.

We hold onto this full firm belief that we deserve more than this. That we deserve normal life where we are considered humans with equal rights, and it's not a luxury.

Throughout my life, I've heard this mantra: "الموت و لا المذلة".

Death over humiliation. Repeated by my parents, my grandparents, great grandparents, and even written on walls

I didn't fully understand it, not until now.

Now I see it in every moment we refuse to bow.

Now I feel it in my bones when I wake up still breathing, resisting when I am not quite sure why, but it's something we do out of nature.

There must be a word more violent than humiliation for what we're enduring. If there isn't one, I'll invent it.

Because this is not life. This is survival on a planet that has decided we are inconvenient.

And we will never forget that.

For over twenty months, this genocide has unfolded in slow, unbearable detail. And the world has learned nothing.

Not your artists. Not your leaders. Not your influencers with their empty slogans and staged heartbreak.

Normalizing and commercializing a genocide where every massacre is used to create "new art," "a new poem," etc. The most controversial omission is that the words of "activists" who condemn the Resistance gain more traction than the people through the genocide.

We are watching. We are recording. We are remembering.

And when this ends, if we survive, we will not applaud your late grief.

We will ask: where were you?
There is no forgiveness in this kind of clarity.
Only the unshakable knowledge that we were right to resist.
That we were never wrong to scream.
That we will never kneel. Not even for your sympathy.
"Still wondering which of the buggers to blame."

— Yara

FRAGILE TRAP

As for being Palestinian, especially Gazan, life always presents more challenges than most can imagine. Life in Gaza demands more endurance than anyone should ever be asked to summon.

I firmly think that my identity would have been different if I weren't Palestinian. I feel a sense of obligation and responsibility to my future self and to our way of life that weighs heavily on me. This is another thing that makes me question if the years I'm living are being wasted. I wonder if all my efforts and the words I write have changed anything, or if I remain, still, at the bottom: colorless, grey.

The world's perception of me is solely based on my origin, which explains why, if someone were to ask me to describe myself, I say "Palestinian." I mold everything around me to reflect that truth, with one glaring exception. I stated that I truly perceive the world in black and white, and that's why I felt grey.

Palestinians can't be filled with someone else's favorite color scheme; they are not coloring books. The world dictates to us, and every other reality is just a variation of that.

Our attempts to emerge from this shell are met with denial. Denial, indeed. But this does not lessen the uniqueness of our experience; rather, it is a cry for acceptance of who we are, not the anguish we endure.

In Palestinian culture, nothing is more contemptible than stealing—be it life, land, or identity.

Life moves by forces beyond our control. Taking any step forward, beyond imposed limits, requires immense courage—a courage that defines the Gazan spirit. This courage teaches me that every moment matters, that even when choices are scarce, we must take the time we deserve to rethink and always hold ourselves accountable.

Personally, I have often felt excluded. But with each step forward I take now, it is for my people, for my family, to give voice to what I call the "naked truth." If I fail, I deserve my exile.

Fyodor Dostoevsky's character Raskolnikov in *Crime and Punishment* is consumed by despair, feeling trapped by fate and forced to accept humiliating punishment.

I can understand how Raskolnikov's sense of despair and disillusionment might resonate with the experiences of someone enduring prolonged conflict. It mirrors a profound existential struggle, one that reflects the feelings of helplessness and futility that can arise in situations of protracted hardship, such as living in a war zone.

For someone in Gaza, the feeling of being trapped in a cycle of suffering with no clear path to a meaningful future can be overwhelming. The idea that life might simply be a series of sacrifices without an ending or a purpose is a poignant parallel to the daily struggles faced by people along the Strip.

The sense of disillusionment with mere existence, as Raskolnikov expresses, might be felt deeply in such circumstances. When our aspirations and dreams seem continually thwarted by external forces, it can lead to a profound questioning of our very purpose and worth. The frustration with a life that feels controlled by forces beyond our actual control can be a source of deep emotional and psychological anguish.

In both cases—whether in the world of Dostoevsky's characters or real-world contexts of adversity—there is a struggle to find meaning throughout our lives. The existential crisis, the feeling that mere survival is insufficient and that we must desire more from life, can be a painful experience. Understanding this can offer a more profound empathy for us when facing such dire situations and might even help us find ways to address and alleviate our suffering.

Palestinian writer Ghassan Kanafani warned: "Don't die before you are a peer."

This metaphor has always driven me forward; it generally describes the dread of dying before I've done all I'm capable of, and it overlooks the limitations of oneself to a set of beliefs and the fact that most people are capable of more than they admit to themselves.

I had always tied myself to my future, and thus, I didn't give much attention to the time and place that required it. Knowing that this might be the stop we make along the way that creates our real lives. For most people, these moments, in particular, despite their harshness, could somehow reveal new and interesting visions of the future that are hidden from us.

But with every breath I take in the wake of death, I realize how far I am from my future because, in the present, I cannot determine whether my dreams are even achievable and whether I can survive.

It takes courage to think beyond the present, but I'm now just waiting for a spark that can illuminate my future. But now it's a matter between me and fate; I can't go forward or back in time; it's just here and now. My future remains vague; all the pieces of the puzzle aren't in place, and all the doors are locked.

However, we must pass through a door that fate has determined.

For as long as time still dares to measure, we have lived through cycles of devastation, watching everything around us collapse while being told to survive. I believed survival was an act of defiance—"shoulders must remain strong." I repeated this like a prayer. However, I now realize that nothing remains intact. No ground solid enough to rebuild upon. This is not recovery; it is a moment when everything has truly fallen apart.

I wish I could write words of hope, as I once did. Something that stretches beyond despair, something that proves we are more than just survivors. But now, all that remains is a despised reality. We who still breathe must recognize ourselves as "dead people walking,"

And behind us, they echo inmates, your time is limited; execution awaits.

The phrase "dead man walking" comes from death row prisons, where inmates hear the grim announcement of their impending fate by wardens, guards, and prison employees. The depressing reminder that an inmate's time is running out and that they might be executed is sent to them by the eerie cries of "dead man walking!" throughout the jail. Gaza has long been called the largest open-air prison in the world, where even daily survival is dictated by oppressors.

Those inmates here survive famine, siege, and violence. On a daily basis, the wardens in their prisons yell, "dead men walking." They would like to yell back, "We did not kill anyone." Being Gazans and wanting to survive is their sole transgression.

Resilience is our inheritance, yet sometimes the spark within flickers toward extinction just when it should be strongest. What does it mean to hold on when your future has been erased, when existence itself feels senseless?

You are left standing between two voids—one where you continue, hollow and aimless, and the other where you cease to be.

So if all they leave me is mere existence, then let death come, let it be my fate—a pain that, at last, relieves. But until that moment, I will remain here, among the ruins, speaking even when my voice is nothing but an echo in a hollowed-out land. If I have to die, let it not be with longing lodged in my throat. Let it not be with my back turned halfway through leaving. Let it not be with my hands still reaching for the unfinished. Because today is a word we no longer believe in.

I don't want to be mourned. Don't grieve for me as if I belonged some-where I was never allowed to stay. We all belong to the dust eventually. But

51

this ground... this ground broke its promise. It was supposed to hold us, but it opened its mouth instead and swallowed. Call this my protest—a refusal to keep pretending this was ever a life. A protest against a world that feeds on its children and calls it survival.

I don't want to go watching the light flicker out behind someone's eyes as their name fades from a mother's lips. I don't want to count the dead with shaking fingers until numbers become the only language I speak.

No. This... this cannot be it. This cannot be what we were made for. But if it is, if death is all that remains untouched, unoccupied, uncolonized—

Then let it come.

Let it arrive not as a thief, but as a final truth.

Let me go, not longing, not unfinished, but refusing. Still refusing.

If they want us to be ghosts, let us haunt them.

— Yara

THE QUIET REVOLT OF A DREAM

Some days, survival feels like betrayal.
Like living is the loudest thing I can do.

Hope isn't loud here.
It's a faint thing, like breathing in sleep—
barely there, but insistent.

Survival no longer resembles life.
It is just continuity.
The machinery of breath.
A resistance born of refusal.

There are mornings I wake up
and grief is already sitting at the edge of the mattress,
waiting...

They've carved a coward out of someone who, not long ago,
stood firmer.

And healing itself doesn't feel like warmth.
It feels like nothing at all.
A numbness dressed as calm.

Meditation
doesn't have the power to silence that sound of a Zannana,
the way it silences my thoughts.

I wish I could outrun my fatigue
the way others do.
I wish I could silence the pain,
and feed the seagulls bread again.
I wish the sea breeze didn't cradle the pain of absence—
tents in place of homes,
a turtle belly-up in the foam.

I wish they knew that when they shoot one down
the rest refuse to kneel
to lift his body with dignity
steadily.
To push his cold body,
or gather her boiling hot chunks,
out of the camera's eye.
To let their father cry shamelessly
and to scream along with their mother.

I wish those kids will not sleepwalk between flames again
and the youth to stay out late
because it was "safe".
I wish I can look into people's eyes again.
I wish we won't sacrifice again,
not that we don't want,
just because we deserve more.

It's strange how memory became a place
and how grief became the slight pause
between an inhale and exhale
after breath vanishes.

To fight that urge to write about dreams.
Noiseless dream
as plain as knowing what day it is.

Paulo Coelho says
It's the possibility of having a dream come true
that makes life...
interesting.

But mine feel like a contraband now
something I have to smuggle past denial,
hidden under my tongue.

Maybe we were never meant to dream.
Maybe we're just the extras
in someone else's film,
the ones who take the hit
so the camera can move on.

But I know I didn't choose this role.
None of us did.

And when they almost convince me
nothing will ever change,
I still write.

Not because it changes anything—
but because if I stop,
the silence will start writing for me.
And I'm afraid of what it might say.

I try to remember the last time I thought of something normal.
A quiet thought,
I had during a nap
I once took with my long black window
slightly open,
wind brushing my Starry Night poster,
when my beige curtain swung
hitting the wall gently.
Strangely, that never bothered me.

Back when I did not consider
our attempts to survive romanticized
gas lighted by our patience.
Back before I owned a small, zipped-tight bag
for dreams I kept folding
smaller and smaller,
so they wouldn't look like threats.

Back when I lovingly picked berries
for my best friend's mum
because they reminded her
of her childhood home.

I place those dreams one by one
in a notebook I never meant to use
the one I packed when I thought
this might be temporary.

We believed this might be temporary.

Finding myself writing stories no one taught me how to tell.
Not the ones with beginnings and ends
those that stretch across bread lines without answers,
where people stand inside cattle cages
held guilty for having empty, grey stomachs,
walking through a fog memory barefoot,
each step crunch of glass beneath waiting
but their footsteps are one way only.
They don't return.

I open my gallery carefully
worried what I'll find inside.

Sometimes it's the look in someone's eyes
when they knew.
When they really knew
we might not come back.

It's like sweeping glass in the dark.
You do it so no one steps
on what already hurt you.

It's strange how memory became a place,
and how grief became something I bump into all the time,
even in silence.
Even when I'm not trying to remember.
It just shows up
in jasmine's scent,
in a sentence,
in the way I wake up too fast
for no reason.

Grief doesn't ask for permission anymore.
It lives here.

Sometimes I wonder
if my body even knows peace.
If it ever really did.
It reacts before I can think now.
To the way we're adapting.

And it's mind blowing
that the hardest part isn't what we've lost.
It's what we were never allowed to have.

It's how normal it started to feel without it.
That we dream quietly.
Half-believing, half-apologizing.
Like maybe dreaming small enough
might let us pass unnoticed.

And still
these aren't "big" dreams.
They wouldn't impress anyone
in the parallel side.

But here,
they are revolutionary.
Just because this place,
this world,
keeps trying to convince us
we were born only to suffer
and that we're strong
because we keep "surviving."

Surviving just enough to keep moving.
And no one asks what it costs.

So I am tired of being strong
if it means never being allowed
to fall apart.

I want to be held
the way people hold old photos
gently, carefully, knowing that
because something bent
doesn't mean it will always be...
broken.

I write like I'm writing to someone I'll never meet,
like this nothingness,
this dull ache

might land on someone's lap across oceans,
and they'll understand
enough to know we mattered.

And I hate that this is what writing became about.
Staying sane,
trying to make sure something is left when all this ends.

Even if I don't always like what comes out.
Even if I have to pause,
delete,
and start again.
Even when it hurts.

Because in a world where stealing remains,
this greedy malicious behavior,
writing is one of the few things
I still get to choose.

And some days,
that has to be enough.

I press my palm to the wall that remains.
It doesn't remember me.
But my hand does.
Trembling.

I carry words in my chest
like small pebbles I collect from ruins.
Some are sharp.
Some are warm.
All of them are smoking.
Quietly undoing everything.

I dream,
not the kind of dreams where I have to be someone,
but those where I simply get to be.
Dreams that slip through a broken window,
onto a dirty street,
marked with coaled fingerprints.

Soft footed,
simply existing,
like the ghosts of what could have been.

I write not because I'm explaining
as if suffering needs to be translated
to be believed.
As if I owe them the right words
before they'll call a massacre a massacre,
before they'll announce the dead deserve to be mourned.

I watch how they witness,
then nod in false sympathy
before turning the channel.

As if the rubble beneath our feet
was never a classroom.
As if their silence isn't violence too.

They ask us to humanize ourselves —
though we've bled proof for decades.

And sometimes I wonder,
do they prefer us in pieces?
Easier to pity that way.
Harder to listen when we're whole.
When our lifeless bodies speak back.
When we demand more than their sadness.

Being dismembered
is not polite enough
without a well-written caption.

But I'm done writing for their comfort.

This is not sympathy.
It is erasure wrapped in fake condolences.
History repeating itself,
pretending it's a debate.

And if Imran's stolen breath
It is not enough to say: enough with the madness,
then let me say it again: enough.

A quiet revolt of a dream,
still breathing
from the wreckage of my humanity,
Because no one came
to kill it yet.

I write because a genocide taught me
there's something sacred
about being the one who remembers.

Even if remembering
breaks you
a little more
each time.

They taught us to mourn
like we were the ones leaving.

The martyr is a beloved.
They taught us to color
the redness of cheeks with dust,
to name love
Only when it becomes lost.

The martyr is a beloved.

The martyr is a beloved.

The martyr is a beloved.

— Yara

WHY WE STILL LOVE GAZA

When I first chose this title, it was not because I had an answer. It was a question I asked out of curiosity. I wanted to know what I have for this love, and why I can't explain it. Why does it feel like excavation?

People sometimes reduce the love for Gaza to the way it was framed, romanticized by poetry, sacrifice, and that kind of loyalty we have to belonging, which sometimes hurts.

Maybe we don't love Gaza because it's safe, "obviously". Maybe Gaza is a mother who cannot protect her children, but they keep going back to her hands anyway. Maybe it's like a house already burning, but you still remember the way it smelled in the morning. You still wait by the window to catch the sunset. You still rush to the sea when you just can't go on.

Maybe this love is just the name you give to the ache. Maybe because you live here in contradiction, you call a place home while it disappears beneath your feet. Because you still stick to the place that could've killed you. Because Gaza didn't offer you a good future, but leaving still feels like exile.

Maybe love isn't the right word. Maybe it's something messier. Something heavier. More like something mysteriously exists.

What happened and what's still happening at least made me realize the moments I knew I loved Gaza.

Because everything around kept proving that we hold yet more love for Gaza. Because its absence would make everything feel colder.

Even when this home swallowed our memories.

Even when it made us old too soon.

It doesn't make sense, right?

It feels like an obligation for something I failed to name, but it brings familiarity. Because the ruins of your room tighten your chest more than a bomb ever will.

I think of the times I wanted to hate this place, when my books were buried, when my loved ones' voices cracked in fear, when my friends' deaths became mere, when our home became a headline, and when the silence that followed was louder than the explosion.

I still don't know why we love Gaza. Maybe because no one else will. Maybe because to stop loving her would mean giving up on ourselves. Maybe I won't ever understand why. Maybe it's something I don't need to explain.

Maybe love is what remains when nothing else does. Or maybe -just maybe — it isn't love at all. Maybe it's an ache. A refusal to stop caring, even when it burns.

This is not an answer. It's what I found when I started asking. Loving Gaza isn't logical.

— Yara

THRESHOLD

The sun relatively is the same, but you're older. Short of breath and one day closer to death. Every year is getting shorter, never seem to find the time.

— Roger Waters, *Time* by Pink Floyd

I once wrote in my journal about how things can disappear without explanation, leaving us blank. That blankness haunts any sense of growth while living in such a place under such conditions. And it somehow mirrors the way Gaza vanishes and reappears in global memory.

There are moments in life when everything appears to be moving in the right direction. You catch your breath, the weight seems a little lighter, and for a fleeting second, you believe... Perhaps it's finally happening. You're okay. But then, without warning, it all begins to fall.

This kind of question doesn't come with a satisfying answer. Why do things fall apart just when we think they're coming together? Is there a force at play we cannot see, some cosmic balance that resents our moments of ease? Or is it just a coincidence dressed in life under occupation?

There are so many questions. Too many, at times. They pile up, refusing to leave. And when no answers come, they begin to shape how we see the world, making confusion feel like the only thing we rely on.

How much of what happens to us is luck? Were we thinking we have control of our lives? Or do our choices shape where we end up? It's easy to believe that choosing to build a life in Gaza might mean we'd at least have control over the bare minimum of our rights. It's much harder when everything collapses in a matter of seconds, and you're left wondering if it was ever real to begin with.

They say that when one door closes, another opens. But no one talks about the hallway in between. And what if that hallway leads nowhere? What if they prevented the next door from even existing, forced us to keep walking in circles, convincing ourselves that motion equals meaning? No one noticed that some of us were born in a room with no door. They didn't notice that some never even had a house.

Life often seems to move on its own terms. It speeds up. Slows down. Turns corners you didn't know were there. And in those turns, everything changes. Your rhythm, your balance, your sense of direction. You try to adjust, but sometimes you're too late.

In those moments, the question becomes: who are we in the middle of all this movement?

In a kind of crisis, it feels like nothing is really happening to us. Rather, we are being moved. Crimes unfold around us, and we simply react. The altitude changes, and suddenly the air feels thinner. What made sense yesterday no longer does. Life spins so fast you forget where the ground is. Your inner self struggles with vertigo. Like you climbed too high, looked down, and forgot how to breathe. And so you fall silent. You stop creating. You stop believing you ever could.

Things disappear, and we don't know why. One day, you are writing. Next, you cannot find the words. One day you're seen. Next, you've vanished.

There's a particular kind of sadness in believing you were never exceptional. That's all you had was timing. Or proximity. Maybe you've been pretending this whole time.

In the wake of such questions, we're left trying to piece together some version of the truth, hoping that somewhere in the asking, we'll stumble onto something solid.

But maybe the point is not to find the answers.

Maybe it's just to keep asking.

And I think now it all comes back to mortality. That you're here, still alive, and someday you won't be. This isn't a debate about existentialism, I am raising my questions and what I see in people.

In this disintegrated society, one can easily question his desires. What does it mean to exist here at all? By simply having this question, you might find that perhaps what you're looking for lies beneath the surface. And you'll realize that this question doesn't have a straightforward answer, especially in such times, you might even need to set it aside.

You think. It gives rise to a feeling, a gesture, a response. But soon, it multiplies. You act without knowing why. You speak with a tone that isn't yours. You begin to live in a pattern shaped by something you never questioned.

But if you stop, if you face the thought and look at it without fear, you'll see it's not untouchable. You can change it. And once you do, the feeling changes. So does the way you carry yourself in a conversation, the way you walk, the way you look at someone from behind the curtain.

Thoughts aren't always truths. Don't rush to believe them. A conclusion is still a thought. And a thought, especially when left unexamined, can grow into something dangerous. It seeps into your subconscious, shapes the way you perceive injustice, how you love, how you surrender or resist.

And here, perhaps, is where the real weight settles: not in the mind alone, but in the soul. Because thoughts don't just pass through. They leave traces. They imprint themselves in the inner silence, where no one else can see. In time, they can darken the spirit, clutter it with noise that sounds like you, but isn't. To cleanse that space and reclaim it is not simply a mental task. It's a spiritual one. It requires courage, yes, but also stillness. The kind that demands you look inward without flinching.

In the end, the danger is not the thought itself, but forgetting you have the right to challenge it. That's how people are conquered, not only by armies, but by the quiet tyranny of their own unchecked minds.

Thousands of high school students in Gaza have been left without any realistic solutions to move forward with what's left of their lives.

And I am still talking about some. Because others became responsible for feeding their families, others were buried, and some do not even dare to think of their future as a priority. They all have no authority to make a decision that could save their future.

The complicity of some is throwing their futures to the wind, simply because they hold no power to decide.

And with every day we remain stuck in this limbo, our lives stay suspended, waiting on the mercy of a ceasefire.

The mercy of our killer.

— Yara

THE STORY IS NOT OVER

We do not know how this story ends.

And maybe that is the point.

This book was never meant to wrap things up in a bow. There is no final scene, no clean conclusion. Gaza does not offer that luxury. Life rarely does.

What we do know is this: we are still here.

Still remembering our homes, even if their walls are gone.

This chapter is not an ending—it is a refusal. A refusal to let our story be reduced to tragedy. A refusal to believe that everything we have been buried. A refusal to let the world move on without carrying something of us with it.

Because this is not over.

There are days we feel like ghosts in someone else's land. Displaced, exiled, disconnected. We carry questions that never find answers. Sometimes, we carry them in the shape of old photos. Sometimes, in the sound of some music we used to hear in Gaza's taxis. Sometimes, in the scent of cardamom in morning coffee reminds us of our kitchen.

But despite everything, we have learned to keep walking.

We have learned that home can be carried inside the body. That memory, when honored, becomes a form of resistance. That storytelling is not weakness—it is breath. It is how we survive without surrendering.

This book came from a place of ache. But it also came from a place of wonder—that we are still able to speak at all. That somehow, between the bombs and the silence, we still believe in words.

And maybe that is what matters now.

Not answers. Not perfection. Not endings, but presence and continuations.

We wrote this book to remember it honestly. To stretch a thread between the rubble and the diaspora. To say: this is how it felt. This is what was lost. This is what still lives.

The story is not over because the wounds still bleed.

Because the buildings may fall, but the voices do not.

The story is not over because the sea still calls our names.
Because children still dream of birthdays.
Because someone, somewhere, still grows tomatoes in a broken backyard.
Still hangs laundry in the sun.
Still writes poems on the back of grocery receipts.

We do not know what tomorrow will look like.
But we know that today, we spoke.
And that is enough—for now.

Let this chapter not be an end, but a door.
A door left open for memory, for return, for rebuilding.
A door that says to you, the reader:

We are not finished.
We are not forgotten.
And we are not alone.

Because the story of Gaza is still unfolding.
And you—if you are willing—are part of what comes next.

— Tareq

TO THE READER

You have made it to the end.
But this is not the end.

If our words stayed with you—even one line, even one image—then we have
done what we came here to do.

This book is not just about Gaza.
It is Gaza.
Its voice, its ache, its stubbornness, its pulse.

If you feel heavy now, good. That weight is not meant to crush you.
It is meant to be carried forward into your thoughts, your conversations,
and your choices.
Not as guilty. But as for responsibility. As a reminder.

Gaza is not gone.
But it needs you. To keep its name alive.

So go.
Tell someone.

About the things that never made it into the news. About the streets we
named. The dreams we chased. The wounds we carry.

If we disappear from your timeline tomorrow, do not let us disappear
from your memory.
If our names are forgotten, remember our words.
If our future is stolen, make sure someone still writes us into history.

That is all we ask of you.

Not to save us.
But to see us.

Not to fix everything.
But to refuse to forget.

Thank you for making it this far.

Now, carry us with you.
So people know,

We lived.
We mattered.

And we still do.

Sometimes, the words retreat.

I questioned why I was doing it at all. I wonder if the prophets still wander these broken streets, or if they too are lost in the labyrinth of our waiting, neither distant nor near, perhaps watching, perhaps silent, asking their questions in shadows.

Or maybe they have become the shadows

fading between the cracks of this fractured sky.

Faith is a quiet companion here, not a blaze but a steady ember, burning softly beneath the ash.

Who will answer when heaven forgets our names? Who will carry the weight when the walls grow too heavy to bear?

No answers arrive. No sky breaks open. Only the cold edge of waiting.

Knock. The question waits in the dust: Why didn't you knock?
    Why didn't you break the walls?

So...

Knock. Knock. Loud.

We do not know the way.

Writing is the knocking itself.

If we wane, this could die.

If we wait, this could die.

If we move, this could die.

Eyes move, this can die.

Come on

Knock.

A bruise on the glass. A trace of someone who refused to disappear.

Don't ask us to explain this. It is what it is.

A gesture toward something unseen.

A promise without a face.

A prayer without words.

—Yara & Tareq

Tareq AlSourani, 17, was born and raised in Gaza City, where he endured the profound pain and hardship of multiple hostilities. Following the latest war on Gaza, six months later, Tareq and his family—his mother and three siblings—left their home, first seeking refuge in Egypt and eventually resettling in Canada. This book marks Tareq's debut as a writer, driven by his belief in the transformative power of storytelling. His writing reflects a deep longing to preserve the truths of his experiences—not just the events themselves but the emotions and lived realities that accompanied them. For Tareq, this book is much more than a chronicle of war. It is a deeply personal homecoming etched onto its pages—a way to express himself from exile while staying intimately connected to the city he was forced to leave. To Tareq, writing is an act of reclamation, both deeply personal and profoundly universal—as he reclaims memory, identity, and hope.

Yara Nasser is an 18-year-old writer and student who grew up—and continues to live—in Gaza City, Palestine. She views writing as something akin to a bellybutton, connecting her to a personal identity molded by rupture, resistance, and reflection. Her interest in journalism and literature informs a mode of storytelling and war memorialization concerned less with representation than with witnessing, always seeking to stay as close to reality as possible. For her, writing is not merely catharsis, but a practice of excavation of truth, dignity, selfhood, and interior life in contexts where all are endangered. She writes to explore the emotional weight of survival and the fragile shape of identity. This book marks the beginning of her journey as a writer, but its roots reach far deeper into her lived experience.

EU Safety Information
Publisher: Daraja Press, PO BOX 99900 BM 735 664 Wakefield, QC J0X 0C2, Canada
info@darajapress.com | https://darajapress.com
EU Authorized GPSR Representative: Easy Access System Europe – Mustamäe tee 50,
10621 Tallinn, Estonia, gpsr.requests@easproject.com
For EU product safety concerns, please contact us at info@darajapress.com

www.ingramcontent.com/pod-product-compliance
Lightning Source LLC
Chambersburg PA
CBHW062104270326
41931CB00013B/3205